CW0037Ø137

GEMS RESET

&

BUTTONS POLISHED

Produced by John Henson
for
ONE for Christian Renewal

© John Henson 1999.
Please note, John Henson accords with the practice of 'ONE' in having a relaxed attitude to his own material with regard to copyright. The prayers and hymns in this book may be copied, reproduced, amended, improved, used freely in worship etc. by churches and groups without seeking permission. Acknowledgements would be appreciated.

ISBN 0 9526792 2 1

Cover design by Keith Spence.

Printed by Stantonbury Parish Print
6 Stable Yard, Downs Barn, Milton Keynes MK 14 7RZ

'ONE FOR CHRISTIAN RENEWAL'

ONE is a network of radical, ecumenical Christians, believing the churches require to adopt more inclusive principles in their quest for unity and more progressive responses to contemporary issues. Information may be gained from the membership secretary, Roger Morbey, 5 Leeds Place, Derby DE1 2RX.

About ~ JOHN HENSON

John Henson is a native of Cardiff and a son of the Manse. He graduated in history and theology at the universities of Southampton and Oxford respectively and was ordained to the Baptist Ministry at Carmel Baptist Church, Pontypridd in 1964. He was responsible for the formation of Pontypridd United Church, a union between his own church and the United Reformed Church in 1969, and played a similar role from 1992-4 when he chaired the steering committee which brought about Canton Uniting Church, Cardiff, on the same basis. He taught history at Cardiff High School from 1970-1973 and then returned to Pontypridd United Church as associate minister with special responsibility for an ecumenical experiment on a housing estate in cooperation with the Anglican communion. Since 1980 he has largely been free-lance, especially acting as pastoral befriender to people in minority groups, including criminal offenders. He continues to assist the ministry in Baptist, United Reformed and Presbyterian churches. He is a former Chairperson of ONE, with interests including left-wing politics, penal reform, peace, inclusive worship and educating the churches towards a positive appreciation of the sexual revolution. He has lectured on faith and gender issues in Strasbourg and Oslo at the invitation of the European Union and the World Student Christian Federation and at universities in Wales. He teaches the piano, plays the cello and organ, gardens, knits and plays badminton. He is happily married to Valerie, his partner for thirty-five years. He has three adult children, Gareth, Iestyn and Rhôda, who assisted him in translating some of the material into Welsh, and to date five grandchildren- Aidan, Bleddyn, Carys, Gwenllian and Dyfrig.

About this Volume.

'Gems Reset and Buttons Polished" arose out of the concern of many members of ONE (One for Christian Renewal) who find it difficult to join in the traditional prayers and hymns of the churches with honesty since the words no longer accurately express their genuine Christian beliefs and commitment. Yet at the same time is felt a sense of loss which is more than just nostalgia for the tools of devotion of fomer years. Is there something which can be rescued from these hymns and prayers? The tunes, surely. But are the words all dross? Can we strip away the militarism, triumphalism, imperialism, flat-earthism, exclusivism, sexism and sentimentalism in which many of the great hymns and prayers are couched? In this volume we try. Whether we succeed or not, whether there is a market for such a product, time alone will tell. Maybe it will be up to others to do better than we have done. Or perhaps the time has come to let the past go in a way which has not happened before in the history of the Christian Church.

For others this volume may just create a new awareness. The new settings and polishings may get some people to realise for the first time that much of what they say and sing in their churches is twaddle and that by continuing they are slowly sawing through the chord which connects faith with reality. The church which encourages its people to sing over and over again words which do not have the ring of truth is doing something very dangerous. It is endangering its own future, which may be a good thing. But on the way it is damaging the psyche of lovely people, and that is very bad indeed.

This book is dedicated to John Henson's father, Revd. W. Clifford Henson who had a special love for the great hymns and liturgical prayers of the Church and introduced hymns of quality both old and new in all the churches where he ministered. He founded the Gwent English Baptist Singing Festival for this purpose. It was his custom to first sing the tunes to his congregation in the fine tenor voice he retained into his eighties. He believed we were expected by God to use our minds in worship and among his pet hates were songs with trite poetry, shallow theology and weak tunes. He had much to endure on this score. He would certainly have agreed with the purpose of this book. Whether he would have been satisfied with the contents is less certain. We shall have to wait until we see him again to find out.

**'Sing heartily, by all means,
but think carefully about what you're singing.'**

(1 Corinthians 14: 15. 'ONE' translation)

GEMS RESET

GEMS RESET

1a. THE BEAUTY ('The Grace')

The Beauty of Jesus our Leader, the Love of God our Parent, and the Joy of the Spirit our Uniter be with us for ever.

Amen.

1b. YR HARDDWCH

Harddwch Iesu ein Harweinydd, Cariad Duw ein Rhiant a Llawenydd yr Ysbryd ein Unwr a fyddo gyda ni am byth.

Amen.

2a. READY FOR GOD ('Prayer of Humble Access')

Loving God, you know our thoughts, our feelings and our secrets. You accept us as we are. Fuse your Spirit with our minds and passions to make our love real and our thanks sincere. We meet you through Jesus, our Leader

Amen.

2b. BAROD I DDUW

Duw Cariadlon, rwyt ti'n gwybod ein meddyliau, ein teimladau a'n cyfrinachau. Rwyt ti'n ein derbyn fel yr ydym ni. Ffiwsia dy Ysbryd gyda'n syniadau a'n nwydau er mwyn gwironeddu ein cariad a'n diolch. Rydyn ni'n cwrdd â thi trwy Iesu ein Harweinydd.

Amen.

3a.   THE PATTERN PRAYER ('The Lord's Prayer')

Loving God, here and everywhere, help us proclaim your values and bring in your New World. Supply us our day to day needs. Forgive us for wounding you, while we forgive those who wound us. Give us courage to meet life's trials and deal with evil's power. We celebrate your New World, full of life and beauty, lasting forever.

Amen.

3b.   GWEDDI PATRWM

Duw Cariadlon, yma ac ym mhobman, helpa ni ddatgan dy egwyddorion a dwyn i mewn dy Byd Newydd. Maddau inni am dy frifo di, fel y maddeuwn ninnau y rheiny sy'n ein brifo ni. Rho inni ddewrder i ymdopi gyda phrofedigaethau a threchu drwg. Rydyn ni'n dathlu dy Byd Newydd, llawn o fywyd a phrydferthwch, yn parhau am byth.

Amen.

4a. **PASSING ON THE GOODNESS (the Levitical Blessing)**

God cheer you and look after you; God convince you that life is good; God assure you that love is the lasting reality; God satisfy your deepest needs; God give you peace, now and forever.

4b. **TROSGLWYDDO'R DAIONI**

Bydded i Dduw dy lawenhau a'th ddiogelu; bydded i Dduw dy ddarbwyllo mai da yw bywyd; bydded i Dduw dy argyhoeddi mai cariad yw'r realiti parhaol; bydded i Dduw gyflawni dy anghenion dyfnaf; bydded i Dduw rhoi heddwch i ti, yn awr ac am byth.

5a. **FRIENDS NOT SERVANTS (Prayer of St. Ignatius Loyola)**

Teach us, Jesus, to help you all we can; to give without resentment more than we intended ; to love and accept love and cope with its pain; to enjoy work, rest and play; to be friends you can rely on; for your sake and ours.
                    Amen.

5b. **FFRINDIAU NID GWEISION**

Dysg ni, Iesu, i'th helpu di fel y gallem ni; i rhoi myw nac yr ydyn yn bwriadu heb anfodlonrwydd; i garu a derbyn cariad ac ymdopi gyda ei phoen; i fwynhau gwaith, gorffwys a chwarae; i fod yn ffrindiau dibynadwy; er dy fwyn di ac er ein mwyn ein hunain.
                    Amen

6a. DUET FOR HEAVEN AND EARTH ('The Gloria')

Enjoy God's beauty above and around,
And share God's peace with every living thing.
Our God and eternal Friend,
Mother and Father of all,
We value you, we thank you,
We praise you for your love.

Jesus, faithful likeness of God,
True God, God given as a present to us,
You remove the world's misery and mess:
Help us and comfort us;
you share our full humanity:
We know you listen.

For only you are genuine;
Only you are pure love,
Only you are worth everything else and more;
Jesus, God's character, with the Spirit, God's presence,
The beauty of God for all to enjoy.

6b. DEUAWD Y NEF A'R DDAEAR

Mwynhewch brydferthwch Duw uwchben ac o gwmpas.
Gan rannu tangnefedd gyda phob peth byw;
Ein Duw a'n cyfaill tragwyddol,
Tad a Mam i ni gyd,
Rydyn ni'n dy ganmol di am dy gariad.

Iesu, tebygrwydd fyddlon Duw,
Gwir Duw, rhoddwyd fel anrheg i ni,
Rwyt ti'n cael gwared o druenni a dryswch y byd
Helpa a chysura ni;
Rwyt ti'n rhannu ein anian daearol:
Rydyn ni'n gwybod dy fod ti'n gwrando.

Canys ti yn unig sy'n ddilys,
Ti yn unig sy'n gariad pur;
Ti yn unig sy'n werth popeth a mwy;
Iesu, anian Duw, gyda'r Ysbryd, presenoldeb Duw,
Prydferthwch Duw i ni gyd mwynhau.

4

7a. MARY'S RADICAL SONG ('The Magnificat')

I sense the greatness of God
Who makes my joy complete;
God smiled at me and asked my help,
And everyone will dance with glee
At the wonderful thing happening to me.
What a God!

In every age God aids the good
Upsetting the plans of the arrogant:
See how the powerful fall off their perches!
Honour for the modest, a banquet for the hungry;
The rich get nothing and slink away!
God keeps promises to friends and companions-
Abraham, Hagar, and their like today.

7b. CÂN RADICALAIDD MAIR

Rwy'n teimlo mawredd Duw,
Mae fy hapusrwydd yn gyflawn;
Gwenodd Duw gan ofyn help,
A bydd pawb yn dawnsio a sbri
O achos fy llawenydd i.
Dyna dduw!

Mae Duw yn helpu pobl da ym mhob oes,
Gan rhwystro cynlluniau'r balch:
Gwelwch yr nerthol yn cael eu gwasgaru!
Anrhydedd i'r gwylaidd, gwledd i'r newynog;
Does dim i'r cyfoethog ac mae nhw'n cilio a chywilydd!
Mae Duw yn cadw pob addewid i'w ffrindiau,
Abraham, Hagar, a phobl fel nhw heddiw.

8a.   ZEK'S LYRICS ('The Benedictus')

What a wonderful God, The God of Rebecca, Jacob and Leah!
This God has come to help us and set us free.

The world will be healed by the power of love,
By a descendant of David and Bathsheba.
Those who spoke God's promises were right:
The days of hate and having enemies are passing.

God was generous to our ancestors,
A loyal and reliable friend.
God promised Sarah and Abraham
An end to hostility and fear,
Freedom to worship and serve.

You, little baby, will speak for God;
You will go in front of God's Chosen Leader
And roll out the carpet.
You will tell people their problems are over,
Free of guilt at last.

God is kind and gentle;
God will turn darkness into daylight,
So we can make our way in peace.

8b.   TELYNEGION SACH

Dyna Dduw! Duw Rebeca, Jacob a Lea!
Mae'r Duw yma wedi dod i'n helpu ni ac i'n rhyddhau.

Mae'n iachau y byd; cariad yw'r moddion,
Dysgynydd Dafydd a Bathseba yw'r meddyg.
Roedd rheiny yn cyhoeddi'r addewidion yn iawn:
Mae'r dyddiau casineb a'r gelyn yn mynd.

Roedd Duw yn hael i'n hynafiaid,
Ffrind dibynadwy am byth.
Mae Duw wedi addo i Sara ac Abraham
Diwedd rhyfela ac ofn,
Rhyddid i addoli a gwasanaethu.

Fe siaradat ti, baban bach, ar ran Duw;
Fe ei di o flaen Detholedig Duw
I atgyweirio'r fyrdd.
Fe gyhoeddi di i bobl diwedd eu trafferthion,
Diwedd eu cywilydd

Mae Duw yn garedig ac yn addfwyn;
Fydd Duw yn troi'r tywyllwch yn oleuni
I ni gerdded mewn heddwch.

9a. SIMEON'S GOODBYE ('The Nunc Dimittis')

Now God your helper is ready to move on,
Because I have seen your plan for the world.
Soon the secret will be out,-
New hope for every land,
The greatest event in your people's history.

OR

Your helper, God, moves on content,
Your plans these eyes have seen,
A new day dawns for every land,
Fulfilling Israel's dream.

9b. "HWYL FAWR" ODDI WRTH SIMEON

Nawr, Duw, rwy'n barod i ymadael,
Wedi gweld dy gynllun i'r byd.
Bydd y cyfrinach yn glur cyn ho hir
Gobaith newydd i bob wlad,
Cyfnod enwocaf yn hanes dy bobl.

NEU

Yn nawr mae d'asiant wrth ei fodd,
Rwyf wedi gweld dy gynllun di;
Bydd bore newydd i bob wlad,
Anrhydedd mawr i'n bobl ni.

10a. LAUNCHING PAD ('The Sursum Corda.')

(V=Voice- presider or member/members of congregation; C=Congregation; A=All)

V   Prepare yourselves in mind and mood!

C   We are ready to meet with God!

V   It's time to show our thanks to God.

C   The right response to love is love.

V   Love is the only response and wherever we are and in whatever mood we should show our love for you, Father, Mother, Friend.

A   So, with those who have done it before and with those who are doing it now, lovingly we thank you and welcome you among us.
Good, wise and beautiful is the Lover of Millions. Life and love is proof of your presence. God above praise, we celebrate because of you.

10b. PAD LANSIO

(L=Llais; C Cynulleidfa; P=Pawb)

L   Byddwch yn barod mewn meddwlfryd ac hwyl!

C   Rydyn ni'n barod i gwrdd â Duw!

L   Mae'n bryd i ni ddangos ein diolch i Dduw.

C   Cariad yw'r ateb iawn i gariad

L   Cariad yw'r unig ateb a ble bynnag rydyn ni a beth bynnag ein hwyl, fe ddylen ni ddangos ein cariad i ti, Tad, Mam, Ffrind.

P   Felly, yng ghwmni rhai sy wedi ei wneud yn y gorffenol ac yng ghwmni rhai sy'n ei wneud yn awr, rydyn ni'n diolch i ti gyda chariad, gan dy groesawu yn ein plith.
Da, call a phrydferth yw'r Carwr Miliynau. Bywyd a chariad sy'n profi dy bresenoldeb. Duw sydd y tu hwnt i ganmoliaeth, rydyn ni'n dathlu o'th herwydd.

11a. GIVING CREDIT WHERE CREDIT'S DUE. ('TE DEUM LAUDAMUS')

We praise you, God:
You are greater than everything.

The whole world marvels
At the one who loves forever.

All those close to you sing your praise:
Their songs echo through time and space.

Artists and musicians
Speak with one voice,-

"Great, wise, and beautiful God,
Lover of millions,

Everywhere your brilliance
Startles and surprises us..'

Those who announce your good news praise you:
Those who speak your words praise you.

Those who have died for you praise you:
Your friends the world over praise you.

All know about your love
Through the one who is your Likeness,
With the help of your Spirit.

Jesus, you are the greatest of all;
You are the true likeness of the Loving God.

To save us from our folly,
You became one of us.

You did away with death and its horrors
And invited everybody to God's New World.

You are one with the being of God.
God's love shines through you.

We believe you will put right
Everything wrong with us.

So your friends look to you for help.
You have made us yours by dying for us.

Help us to be like you
And reflect your beauty.

God, heal your people and improve their lives;
Teach them to love, and inspire them with confidence.

You seem greater to us every moment;
There is always more to learn about you.

Help us today to avoid being selfish;
We are glad you keep on forgiving us.

Your kindness makes us want to please you.
Each says, "I trust you God.
You will not let me down".

11b. RHOI CLOD

Rydym ni'n dy ganmol di, Duw:
Rwyt ti'n fwy na phopeth.

Mae'r holl ddaear yn rhyfeddu
At yr un sy'n caru am byth.

Mae'r rhai sy'n agos atat ti yn canu dy foliant:
Mae'r cerdd yn atseinio trwy amser a gofod.

Mae pob arlunydd a phob cerddor
Yn dweud gyda'r un llais:

"Duw mawr, call a phrydferth,
Carwr miliynau,

Mae dy ddisgleirdeb yn peri
Rhyfedd a syndod ym mhobman."

Mae'r rhai sy'n cyhoeddi dy newyddion da yn dy ganmol di:
Mae'r rhai sy'n siarad dy eiriau yn dy ganmol di:
Mae'r rhai sy wedi marw ar dy gyfer di yn dy ganmol di.
Mae dy ffrindiau dros y byd yn dy ganmol di.

Fe ddaw yr holl bydasawd i wybod am dy gariad di,
Drwy dy Debygwrydd, gyda chymorth dy Ysbryd.

Iesu, ti sy'n fwyaf o bawb;
Ti sy'n debygrwydd gwir y Dduw cariadlon.

Er mwyn ein achub ni o'n ffolineb,
Fe ddest ti'n un ohonon ni.

Wedi trechu marwolaeth a'i arswydau,
Dyna ti'n gwahodd bawb i'r Byd Newydd Duw.

Rwyt ti'n un gyda bodolaeth Duw.
Mae cariad Duw yn tywynnu drwyot ti.

Rydyn ni'n credu dy fod di'n mynd
I atgyweirio bopeth sy'n ddrwg ynom ni.

Felly rydyn ni'n edrych arnat ti am gymorth,
Dy ffrindiau di trwy gyfrwng dy angau ar ein cyfer.

Helpa ni fod yn debyg i ti
Gan adlewyrchu dy brydferthwch.

Duw, iacha dy bobl a gwellha eu bywydau;
Dysg iddynt garu a rho hyder iddynt.

Rwyt ti'n ymddangos yn fwy i ni pob eiliad;
Mae'n wastad rhagor i'w ddysgu amdanat ti.

Helpa ni heddiw i osgoi fod yn hunanol;
Rydym ni'n llawen am dy fod ti'n dal ati i'n maddau.

Mae dy garedigrwydd yn ein hannog ni i dy blesio di:
Dywed pob un, "Rwy'n ymddiried ynot ti, Duw.
Fyddi di ddim yn fy siomi i.

Buttons Polished

Buttons Polished

1. **BRING TO GOD** (after 'Praise my soul')

(1)   Bring to God a load of presents;
Write 'With Thanks' and wrap with care;
- thanks for status, health, acceptance,
Benefits we have to share.

        God is Special, God is Special,
        Advertise it everywhere!

(2)   Think what God did for our comrades
In the days of history,
When in trouble, need, rejection,
Gave them hope and set them free.

        God is Special, God is Special,
        Sheer dependability.

(3)   We are certain as the weather
Sun today, tomorrow rain;
This brief life we, Oh, so careless,
Undervalue, to our shame.

        God is Special, God is Special,
        Mourns our loss and shoulders our blame.

(4)   We possess the ideal parent-
Mother, father, all in one;
Gently from our worst restrains us,
Heartens with a warm "well-done!"

        God is Special, God is Special,
        Always there and full of fun.

P.T.O.

(5)   Help us, all you others out there,
Celebrate the one we name.
You can come to our opinion
Of the love always the same.

God is Special, God is Special,
Delivers the goods, deserves the fame.

(After HF. Lyte. Best to the tune 'Regent's Square'.)

2.   JUST LIKE A SHEPHERD

(1)   Just like a shepherd in olden times,
       My Leader shows the way,
       And finds the quiet spots to rest,
       Where shimmering waters play.

(2)   My spirits lift in such company;
       I find the strength to walk
       The paths of justice and of peace,
       Even though the cynics mock.

(3)   I'll even count my life's breath cheap
       And face that dark ravine;
       I'll follow still the steady staff
       And tred the way it's been.

(4)   The table's set to celebrate:
       The enemy's looking glum -
       With pleasing touch and healing scents
       Are served the food and wine.

(5)   There's not a lot that can go wrong
       If in that Love I stay;
       With present friends and those to come
       I'll venture, rest and play.

2b.   Fel Bugail Amser Maith Yn ôl

(1)   Fel bugail amser maith yn ôl,
       Yr Iesu f'arweinydd yw,
       A ffindio'r llefydd mwyaf hardd
       Gerllaw yr dyfroedd byw.

(2)   Codwyd fy hwyl gan ffrind o'r fath,
       Mae geni'r nerth a'r nawdd
       I fynd ar llwybrau iawn a syth
       Yn wyneb sbeit a gwawd.

(3)   Fe berygla'm mywyd hyd yn oed,
       A mentro du y cwm,
       Tu ôl i'r Iesu mawr pob cam
       Sy'n cario rod a ffon.

(4)   Mae'n amser dathlu wrth y bwrdd,
       Mae'r gelyn yn gwylio'n flin,
       A theimlad serch ac aroglau per
       Fe gaf i bwyd a llyn.

(5)   Does dim i amharu fy llonydd nawr,
       Derbynnydd o'i gariad ef,
       A ffrindiau mawr a miri da,
       Fe rhof fy llafar lef.

                 (Paraphrase of Psalm 23, in the tradition of many such paraphrases)

3. WALK BESIDE ME.

(1) Walk beside me, friend and lover,
Till we make that better land;
Strength and weakness match each other;
Hold me, firm and tender hand.

Spread the table, spread the table-
We will share a banquet grand!.

(2) Meet me at the spring of water
Pure and clean and sparkling too.
Dreams of cloud and fire and thunder
Vanish as I drink with you.

Fill the glasses, fill the glasses,
We will drink to love and joy.

(3) When we reach that chilly river
Conquer my anxiety.
You are Life, - and death's destroyer;
I will share your victory.

Keep me singing, keep me singing,
Now and to eternity.

(After William Williams Pantycelyn - Tune: Cwm Rhondda John Hughes, Pontypridd)

4.   BENEATH THE CROSS OF JESUS

(1)   Beneath the cross of Jesus, as to my home I come,
A rock which gives protecting shade from burning summer sun;
A shelter from the scorching wind, a respite on the way
From the sweltering of the midday heat
And the burden of the day.

(2)   A welcome spot to rest in, proved many times before;
A place where meet the gentle heart and 'rejects' grieving sore;
As Jacob once in olden times a vivid dream was given,
Seems Jesus on the cross to me a ladder up to heaven.

(3)   There lay near that grim hilltop, but on the farther side,
The darkness of an awful void that gaped both deep and wide;
Then raised between us was the cross, two arms outstretched to save,
And now a lovely garden blooms where once there was a grave.

(4)   Upon the cross of Jesus my eyes at times can see
The very dying form of one who suffered there for me;
And from my grateful heart with tears two wonders I confess:
The wonder of his glorious love and my new happiness.

(5)   I mark the cross-shaped shadow as this world's healing place;
No other comfort sweeter than the welcome on his face;
Discarding now all worthless things, I trust, in pain and loss;
My selfish ways my shame; my joy- the one who bore that cross.

(After Elizabeth Clephane, 1830-69)

22

5.   MY GRACIOUS FRIEND

(1)   My gracious friend, you merit well
    Each loving action I can show;
    I own it as my greatest thrill
    Your roles to play, your mind to know.

(2)   What is my being but for you,
    It's sure support, its noblest end,
    Your ever-loving face in view,
    Helping the cause of such a friend?

(3)   I would not seek self-centred joy,
    Or thrive against another's good,
    Nor future days or powers employ
    Spreading a famous name abroad.

(4)   It's for my Leader I would live,
    The one who for my freedom died;
    Nor could a world united give
    More happiness than at his side.

(5)   His work my wrinkled age shall bless
    When youthful vigour is no more.
    And my last hour of life confess
    His love has animating power.

(After Philip Doddridge 1702-51. His hymn begins, 'My gracious Lord, I own thy right
to every service I can pay: And call it my supreme delight to hear thy dictates and obey.')

6. ONWARD CHRISTIAN COMRADES

(1) Onward, Christian comrades,
Jesus shows the way;
With his cross to guide us,
Love will win the day
Face with good each evil,
Wrath with the soft word,
Smile till stonefaced bigots
Meekly drop their guard.
chorus: Onward, Christian comrades...

(2) Feeling for each other,
Freely let us move,
Sisters, brothers, partners
In the cause of love;
Celebrating difference,
Recognizing worth;
No-one is rejected,
No-one trapped by self.
chorus...

(3) Crowns and thrones must perish,
Power-blocks all fall;
One foundation constant,
God's strong love for all;
Ignorance and prejudice
Try to undermine,
God still goes on loving
Past the end of time.
chorus...

(4) Onward, freedom-seekers,
Set your souls at ease;
You will be composers
Of new harmonies
Glory without triumph,
Prize with none's defeat,
First the first-place taking
Washing others' feet.
chorus....

6b YMLAEN CYDYMEITHION

(1) Ymlaen, cydymeithion,
Iesu'n arwain ni,
Gyda'i groes i'n tywys
Cariad fydd o fri;
Gyda da gorfygu
Pob drygioni ddaw,
Gwenwch nes i'r penboeth
Fynd yn deg a thaw.
        Cytgan: Ymlaem, cydymeithion...

(2) Teimlwn am ein gilydd.
Symudwn yn rhydd,
Brodyr a chwiorydd,
Cariad yw einffydd;
Dathlu ein gwahaniaeth,
Gwerthfawrogi oll;
Neb yn cael ei gwrthod,
Dim garcharor goll.   Cytgan..

(3) Coron a theyrnwialen
Wedi mynd o'r ddaer,
Un sylfaen parhaol
Yw ei gariad taer.
Rhagfarn ac anwybod
Ei elynion yw,
Duw o hyd yn caru
Er eu gwaethaf nhw.   Cytgan....

(4) Ymlaen cyd-anturwyr,
A chalonnau llon,
Cyfansoddu'n fedrus
Donau newydd spon;
Clod heb buddugoliaeth,
Enill heb taflu llaid;
Nhw y bydd yn gyntaf
Cyntaf golchi traed.   Cytgan....

(After Sabine Baring-Gould 1834-1924 Tune: St. Gertrude - Sullivan)

7.   NOW THANK WE ALL OUR GOD

(1)   Now thank we all our God,
With hearts and hands and voices,
For such amazing things
In which this world rejoices.
God's loving arms were known
In early days of care;
And countless gifts of love
Show they are always there.

(2)   Since this most generous God
Will all our lives be near us;
Let's culture joyful hearts,
And signs of peace to cheer us;
Then may we feel that hand
To guide us when perplexed,
And face whatever comes
In this world and the next.

(3)   All thanks to God who loves
us evermore, and with it
To Jesus, leader, friend,
who gives the loving spirit;
The ever-lively God
whose praise we gladly sing,
With lives set free and new
as our thank-offering.

(After Martin Rinckart 1586-1649 & Catherine Winkworth 1827-78)

8. ONE THERE IS

(1) One there is above all others,
Well deserves the name of friend.
His is love beyond a mother's,
Costly, free and knows no end:
Those who once his kindness prove,
Find it everlasting love.

(2) Which of all our friends to save us
Could, or would, have shed their blood?
On the cross he died to have us
Friends of his and friends of God.
This was boundless love indeed!
Jesus is the friend we need.

(3) When he lived on earth rejected,
"Friend of outcasts" was his name;
Now above all praise exalted,
To the title he lays claim:
Ever calls them his best friends,
And to all their needs attends.

(4) Could we bear from one another
What he daily bears from us?
Yet this glorious friend and brother
Loves us though we treat him thus;
Though for good we render ill,
Calls us sisters, brothers still.

(5) O for grace our hearts to soften!
Teach us, Leader, how to love.
We, for shame!, forget too often
What a friend you always prove;
But when home we all are brought,
We will love you as we ought.

(John Newton 1725-1807 altered.Tunes: Ml Saints, Gounod or Magister)

9.   COME TAKE YOUR STAND WITH JESUS

(1)   Come, take your stand with Jesus-
The bravest of the brave:
With him announce the Good News,
The power of love to save.
The virtues of the Spirit
You only have to ask:-
The patience and the kindness
To fit you for the task.

(2)   Come, take your stand with Jesus
To music of your choice;
Guitar or drum or organ
Will help you find your voice.
Right now a task awaits you
To match your best desire;
God will supply the wisdom
If you light up the fire.

(3)   Come, take your stand with Jesus
With labelled and condemned;
The righteous well may shun you
If you're the sinners' friend.
Fear not to haunt the venues
Where outcasts entertain;
They do not stand for Jesus
Who are their cause of pain.

(4)   Come, take your stand with Jesus-
He is the coward's mate;
You're not the first to fail him
Or make him patient wait;
He calls not for heroics
Save from the front-line few;
If you are shy or nervous,
He has a place for you!

(5)   Come, take your stand with Jesus;
He always needs more friends;
The heart-ache lasts a short while,
The loving never ends.
And great will be your pleasure
When holding still your place,
He turns aside to greet you
And knows your name and face.

(After 'Stand up! Stand up for Jesus! George Duffield 1818-88. Tune: Morning Light.)

10.　HE IS ALIVE! TIME TO REJOICE

(1)　He is alive! Time to rejoice;
　　　Now is the day to find your voice:
　　　Tell every culture, every creed,
　　　"The one you seek is risen indeed!"

(2)　He is alive! Who then shall fear
　　　To face life's challenges and care?
　　　Or make their feelings truly known
　　　To him who craves no crown or throne?

(3)　He is alive! The verdict stands-
　　　You are set free by nail-pierced hands;
　　　Justice more kind than courts decide,
　　　- a judge who takes the offender's side!

(4)　He is alive! the barriers fall;
　　　The Holy City welcomes all;
　　　Villains and victims, straight and queer,
　　　All now to one another dear.

(5)　One world - a dream beyond all hope
　　　Jesus has brought within our scope;
　　　You know his love, you know his name,-
　　　So sing along and spread his fame!

(After Josiah Conder 1789-1855 'The Lord is King! Lift up thy voice.
Tunes Niagara or Church Triumphant)

29

11.   JESUS, I CLAIM YOUR PROMISE

(1)   Jesus, I claim your promise
      To hold me to the end;
      It's good to know you're near me,
      My leader and my friend;
      I shall not fear life's challenge
      Since you are by my side,
      Nor choose a crooked pathway
      With you to be my guide.

(2)   I want to feel you near me,
      So many choices here;
      The worthless things that dazzle,
      Slick voices in my ear.
      The struggles deep inside me,
      What knocks me all about
      You give me heart to cope with,
      Give purpose to my doubt.

(3)   I often hear you speaking
      With gentle words and still
      Above the noisy music
      With which my head I fill;
      Sometimes you make me hurry,
      Sometimes you slow me down;
      I know your smile's approval,
      And recognize your frown.

(4)   You've cut some tracks before me
      To open up the way;
      The route is marked 'adventure',-
      I'm starting from today.
      Encourage and inspire me,
      Strong love which has no end;
      Prepare your famous welcome,
      My leader and my friend.

(After J.E.Bode 1816-74)

12.   GLADLY I ACCEPT

(1)   Gladly I accept and humbly,
       God is known in many ways;
       Here on earth a man called Jesus
       Showed us God with human face.

(2)   Hate was on the cross defeated,
       Evil lost its power to cling;
       Mighty love which won that victory
       Is my guide in everything.

(3)   As each day the more I love him,
       More upon my heart I take;
       For themselves I cherish others -
       Even more for his dear sake.

(4)   I with my unique experience
       Meet his many other friends,
       And we share not rule or dogma
       But the love that never ends.

(5)   Great must be the appreciation
       I can never give alone,
       God the Spirit, God the human,
       God the many and the One.

(After John Henry Newman 1801-90 Tunes: Shipston or Sharon)

13. AMAZING GRACE

(1)   Amazing grace (how sweet the sound!)
That saw the worth in me;
I once was lost, but now am found,
Was blind, but now I see.

(2)   When ignorance ruled by fear in me
Then grace my fears removed;
How great that hour of setting free-
To know that I was loved!

(3)   'Spite accident and foolish choice
I have survived thus far;
'Grace',- 'Love-in-action', had a voice
Or I would not be here.

(4)   Good things are what Love promised me
And I trust what Love says;
The God of grace my help will be
Now and for all my days.

(After John Newton 1725-1807)

14. THOSE WHO ARE DOWN

(1)   Those who are down need fear no fall,
      Those who are low no pride;
      Those who are humble always will
      Have God close by their side.

(2)   Let's be content with what we have,
      Unless it is too much;
      Then we should try to shed the load
      Lest conscience lose its touch.

(3)   "Carry no pack", our Leader said;
      "Whether of goods or care."
      My venture will full strength require,
      Joy is for those who dare."

(4)   Jesus, life was for you so rough
      Yet you found ease of mind,
      Teach us the secret in our day
      When peace is hard to find.

(5)   Help us to mind not what we lose
      Or what we fail to gain,
      Give thanks for comforts real and not
      Make too much of our pain.

(6)   Thank you for giving each our cross;
      We could not shoulder yours;
      As someone helped you bear its weight,
      You gladly help with ours.

(7)   Those who are down need fear no fall;
      You greet them, "Come on up!"
      Those who are humble sit, amazed,
      To share your food and cup.

(After John Bunyan 1628-88 Tune: Arden or St. Bernard)

33

15. DEAR SPIRIT OF GOD (Veni Creator Spiritus)

(1) Dear Spirit of God, our hearts inspire,
And warm and light them with your fire;
You are the drink our fervour lifts;
You shower us with such precious gifts.

(2) When sick, with healing balm you soothe;
You make our weary muscles move;
And as we grope to find our way
You shine a torch as bright as day.

(3) Blow fierce strong wind, knock barriers down;
Relax the good with singer and clown;
Then gentle, female dove proclaim
That peace which seasoned lovers claim.

(4) Escort us to the home of God;
There show us how you play your part;
You Son and Father interface
And complement with mother's grace.

(doxology) Praise life and love and power and voice,
Beauty and feeling, thought and choice.

16.   THE SON OF GOD ADVENTURES OUT

(1)   The Son of God adventures out
       A hero's fame to win;
       His rainbow banner waves aloft,
       Who dares to follow him?
       Who dares to drink his offered cup
       With love filled to the brim?
       Who dares to take a rough cross up?
       Who dares to follow him?

(2)   Steven it was whose angel eye
       Could pierce beyond the grave;
       He saw his leader in the sky
       And called on him to save;
       Like Jesus, pardon on his tongue,
       As murderers crowded in,
       He prayed for those who did the wrong;
       Who dares to follow him?

(3)   Courageous band, at first a few,
       On whom the Spirit came;
       Brave or alarmed, their hope they knew,
       And mocked the cross and flame.
       They faced the angry soldier's steel
       And in the lion's den
       They bowed their necks the death to feel;
       Who dares to follow them?

(4)   Eternal friends, from every strand
       Of rich humanity,
       They now around their leader stand,
       A merry company;
       They climbed the steep ascent of heaven
       Through peril, pain and sin;
       O God, may love to us be given
       Who dare to follow them.

(After Reginald Heber 1783-1826. The Son of God goes forth to war.)

17.   WHEN WE'VE CHRIST AS OUR FRIEND

(1)   When we've Christ as our friend
And his words we attend,
What a pleasure we share and display;
While together we plan,
And each does what they can
To help the New World on its way.

Chorus: Smile and be free,
Say, "I'm glad to be me!",
We're the friends- and not servants-
Jesus wants us to be.

(2)   Many shadows will rise;
There'll be clouds in the skies,
And they won't always go the same day;
There'll be doubting and fears
And a fair share of tears,
But our friend holds us tight all the way.

(3)   And the closer we walk
And the more that we talk,
The greater the friendship will be;
If no faults are forgiven
There's no love in return,
So don't hide from the one who can see.

(4)   There'll be good times as well,
And great stories to tell
With plenty of fine company;
Then we'll see God's World come
And we'll feel quite at home
When those bright merry eyes we first see.

(After J.H. Sammis 1846-1919 'Trust and Obey')

18.   JESUS COMES

(1)   Jesus comes, with streamers flying,
      Once as friend of outcasts killed;
      Crowds of keen supporters with him,
      Mouths with joyful laughter filled
            loudly cheering (x3)
      Ears and eyes and hearts are thrilled.

(2)   There's no mistaking this time round;
      Perfect love now understood;
      We who spat and sent him bound,
      Broken, to a cross of wood,
            truly sorry (x3)
      Glad that wrath is not his mood.

(3)   Dare we look or shyly glance
      At that body full of grace?
      Marks of thorns and nails and lance,
      Sorrow lingering on his face?
            Brightly smiling! (x3)
      All our anxious fears give place.

(4)   Humble Jesus, same as ever,
      Spurns a throne of grand design;
      Loving always, judging never;
      Towel and basin still the sign;
            You will be with us (x3)
      When we greet the end of time.

(5)   Merriment and quiet worship
      Mingle as we work and wait;
      For it is no tyrant lordship
      We with dread anticipate;
            Ours is the hurry (x3)
      He'll be not a moment late.

                  (After Charles Wesley. Tune: Helmsley)

37

19.   FOR SPLENDID FOLK

(1)   For splendid folk who have gone home to God.
        Those who on earth life's pavements finely trod,
        And whose example gladly we applaud,
        Praise to their memory
        While still we journey.

(2)   You taught them love, its way, its truth, its life,
        Jesus, God's Likeness, answer to earth's strife;
        Reason their tool, replacing gun and knife,
        Praise to their memory
        While still we journey.

(3)   May we, like them, be in our thinking bold,
        Leaving behind the patterns worn and old,
        Drawn on by wisdom's gleam, not that of gold,
        Praise to their memory
        While still we journey.

(4)   The day will come when we with them unite,
        All in new clothing, colours gay and bright;
        Darkness at last defeated, only light,
        Sharing our memories
        Of all our journeys.

                        (After W.W. How 1823-97 'For all the Saints')

20. REJOICE AND CELEBRATE

(1) Rejoice and celebrate,
Your Friend and Leader cheer;
Sing, decorate and dance,
And in his victory share.
Prepare yourself in mind and voice,
Let bright emotions flow, REJOICE.

(2) Jesus, our hero, lives
To spread God's love and peace;
Guilt and self-hatred fade
And hope and trust increase.
Prepare yourself in mind and voice,
Let confidence return, REJOICE.

(3) Put failure from your thoughts;
God's New World is in sight;
All deathly negatives
Jesus has put to flight.
Prepare yourself in mind and voice,
Say 'Yes' to life and fun, REJOICE.

(4) The story has no end,
We look for more and more;
The love that's given so much
Still has a well-packed store.
Prepare yourself to hear love's voice
And see the face of God, REJOICE.

(After Charles Wesley. Tune: Darwall)

21.

Grace

(For meals. May be used at Communion)

Jesus, we join you at your board;
Be here and everywhere adored;
These good things share, and grant that we
Your banquet full may one day see.

(rewriting of grace, 'Be present at thy table, Lord'
-usually sung to tune Rimington.)

Dweud Diolch

Iesu, ymunwn wrth y bwrdd;
Croeso i bawb, gyrwyd neb iffwrdd;
Rhannu ein bwyd a diolch wnawn,
Yng ngobaith gweld dy wledd yn llawn.

INDEXES.
Index to Prayers.

Buttons (Hymns)

BOOKS BY JOHN HENSON

Other Communions of Jesus (1994) ISBN 0 9526792 1 3
The communal meal stands at the centre of worship in most Christian traditions.
But have we been doing it right?

Price £5 + 75p p&p

The Bad Acts of the Apostles (1996) ISBN 0 9526792 0 5
An unusual approach to the study of Acts.

Price £4.50 + 75p P&p

The 'ONE' Translation of the New Testament.
(Translation coordinator: John Henson)

A new concept in the translation of the scriptures in which all can share. Fresh,
vibrant, contemporary, non-academic, nonsexist, different.

Already available: Mark (£1); Romans/James (£1); Hebrews (£1); John (£1.50);
Acts (£2); Letters to the Corinthians (£2). Further volumes in preparation.
Reductions for orders of the complete current set and for bulk orders.

From: John Henson,
             2 Sycamore Street,
             Taffs Well,
             Cardiff.
             CF4 7PU